THE GREAT BIBLE
DISCOVERY

ELIJAH AND ELISHA

THE BIBLE IS A BEST-SELLER. IT IS ALSO ONE OF THE MASTER-WORKS OF WORLD LITERATURE - SO IMPORTANT THAT UNIVERSITIES TODAY TEACH 'NON-RELIGIOUS' BIBLE COURSES TO HELP STUDENTS WHO CHOOSE TO STUDY WESTERN LITERATURE.

THE BIBLE POSSESSES AN AMAZING POWER TO FASCINATE YOUNG AND OLD ALIKE.

ONE REASON FOR THIS UNIVERSAL APPEAL IS THAT IT DEALS WITH BASIC HUMAN LONGINGS, EMOTIONS, RELATIONSHIPS. 'ALL THE WORLD IS HERE.' ANOTHER REASON IS THAT SO MUCH OF THE BIBLE CONSISTS OF STORIES. THEY ARE FULL OF MEANING BUT EASY TO REMEMBER.

HERE ARE THOSE STORIES, PRESENTED SIMPLY AND WITH A MINIMUM OF EXPLANATION. WE HAVE LEFT THE TEXT TO SPEAK FOR ITSELF. GIFTED ARTISTS USE THE ACTION-STRIP TECHNIQUE TO BRING THE BIBLE'S DEEP MESSAGE TO READERS OF ALL AGES. THEIR DRAWINGS ARE BASED ON INFORMATION FROM ARCHAEOLOGICAL DISCOVERIES COVERING FIFTEEN CENTURIES.

AN ANCIENT BOOK - PRESENTED FOR THE PEOPLE OF THE SECOND MILLENNIUM. A RELIGIOUS BOOK - PRESENTED FREE FROM THE INTERPRETATION OF ANY PARTICULAR CHURCH. A UNIVERSAL BOOK - PRESENTED IN A FORM THAT ALL MAY ENJOY.

M publishing
CARLISLE, UK

10

During Solomon's reign many people had felt discontented, because of the high taxation and forced labour imposed on them. When his son Rehoboam refused to lighten their burden, the old split between the northern tribes and the southern ones reopened. The prophets of the Lord supported Jeroboam, the new king. The new state of affairs had important religious consequences. Jeroboam, the new king of the Northern Kingdom (Israel), decided it was important to reduce contact with the Southern Kingdom (Judah). So he set up two new temples in the north and south of his kingdom (Dan and Bethel). Here worshippers found images of bulls - 'the gods who led us out of Egypt'.

Under a later king, Ahab, there was even a danger that the God of Israel would be replaced by the god of Phoenicia. Possibly this would have happened apart from the courage of the prophet Elijah. He saved what remained of the true faith of Israel. His successor and helper, Elisha, seems to have been a far gentler person than Elijah. Like the older prophet, he was remembered as a miracle-worker, but Elisha had far more contact with ordinary people. He also trained younger men as prophets. It is no accident that almost all of the miracles recorded in the Old Testament are placed in this period and at the time of the exodus. Both were crises in the history of God's people.

Life in Israel was often unsettled. One reason was that it had no royal dynasty. Judah remained loyal to the house of David. But Israel experienced one coup after another. A 'strong man' would seize power, then his son would be the victim of another revolution. In addition, both kingdoms were now liable to be invaded by Egypt or Assyria. The security of David's reign was over. These were troubled times.

1 & 2 Kings

ELIJAH AND ELISHA

10

First published as *Découvrir la Bible* 1983

First edition © Larousse S.A. 1984
24-volume series adaptation by Mike Jacklin © Knowledge Unlimited 1994
This edition © OM Publishing 1995

01 00 99 98 97 96 95   7 6 5 4 3 2 1

OM Publishing is an imprint of Send the Light Ltd.,
P.O. Box 300, Carlisle, Cumbria CA3 0QS, U.K.

Introductions: Peter Cousins

British Library Cataloguing in Publication Data
A catalogue record for this book is available from the British Library
ISBN 1-85078-214-8

Printed in Singapore by Tien Wah Press (Pte) Ltd.

ELIJAH
THE PROPHET

DAN

SHECHEM

SHILOH

BETHEL

Jordan

JERICHO

JERUSALEM

HEBRON

BEERSHEBA

Mediterranean Sea

SCENARIO: Etienne DAHLER
DRAWING: Victor de la FUENTE

AFTER SOLOMON HAD DIED, THE BAD FEELINGS BETWEEN THE NORTHERN AND SOUTHERN TRIBES FLARED UP AGAIN.

JEROBOAM, WHO HAD BEEN ONE OF SOLOMON'S OFFICIALS, RUSHED BACK FROM EGYPT, WHERE HE HAD TAKEN REFUGE...

...WHILE **REHOBOAM** WAS GETTING READY TO BE CROWNED KING.

REHOBOAM, THE NORTHERN TRIBES WANT YOU TO BE ANOINTED AT SHECHEM.

RIGHT! IF THAT IS WHAT THEY WANT!

GO HOME, KING OF JUDAH!

REHOBOAM, YOU WON'T BE KING OVER ISRAEL!

THE REBELLION WAS SO GREAT THAT REHOBOAM HAD TO FLEE TO JERUSALEM.

I WILL HAVE MY REVENGE!

GATHER TOGETHER ALL THE MEN OF JUDAH AND BENJAMIN!

YOUR MAJESTY, BEFORE YOU GIVE ORDERS, YOU HAD BETTER SEE WHAT IS HAPPENING IN THE PALACE SQUARE.

THE GOD OF ISRAEL SAYS THIS: 'DON'T ATTACK YOUR BROTHERS! WHAT HAS HAPPENED IS MY WILL!'

SHEMAIAH IS A MAN OF GOD; YOU SHOULD LISTEN TO HIM.

GOOD! I SHALL WAIT!

JEROBOAM FORTIFIED SHECHEM AND LIVED THERE.

THE NORTHERN TRIBES MADE JEROBOAM KING OF ISRAEL. THE BREAK BETWEEN NORTH AND SOUTH WAS COMPLETE.

THE PEOPLE MUSTN'T GO TO **JERUSALEM!**

BUT... THE **TEMPLE IS THERE!**

VERY WELL! WE WILL BUILD PLACES FOR WORSHIP ON THE BORDERS OF THE KINGDOM.

JEROBOAM ORDERED TWO LARGE PLACES OF WORSHIP TO BE BUILT, ONE AT BETHEL, THE OTHER FURTHER NORTH AT DAN. THERE THE PEOPLE OFFERED SACRIFICES TO THE GOLDEN BULLS.

YOU ARE BLESSED, YOU WHO BROUGHT US OUT OF EGYPT.

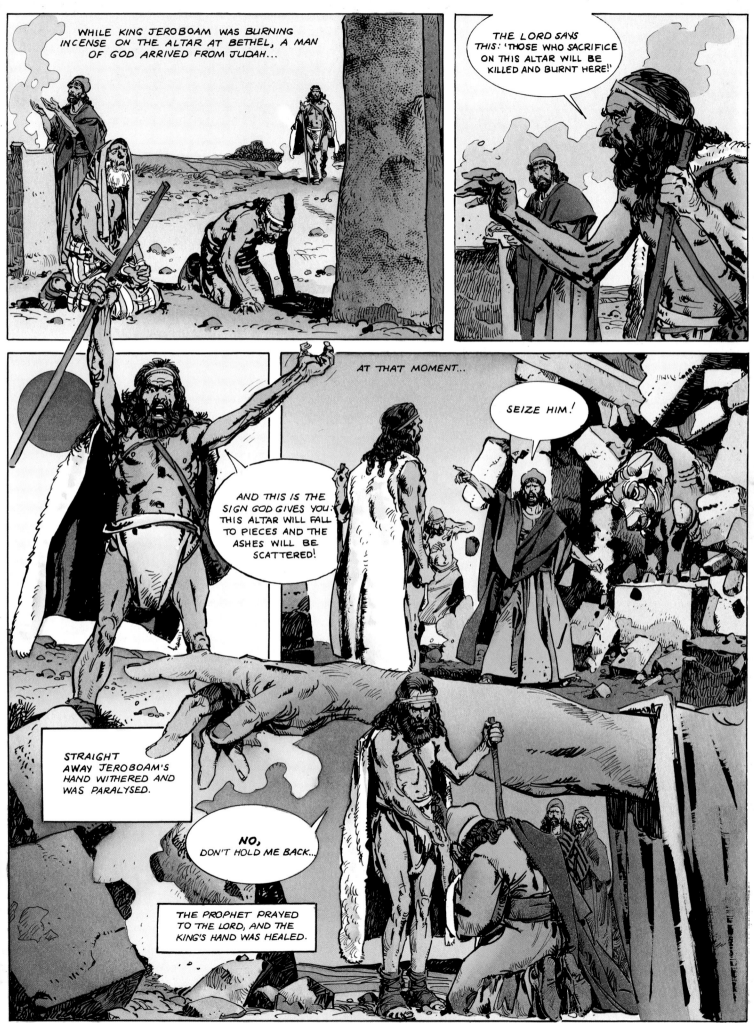

IN THE KINGDOM OF JUDAH THEY WERE DANCING IN FRONT OF THE IDOLS.

THE PHARAOH IS INVADING!

IN THE FIFTH YEAR OF REHOBOAM'S REIGN SHESHONQ, THE KING OF EGYPT, ATTACKED JERUSALEM AND TOOK EVERYTHING AWAY.

LORD PHARAOH, HERE ARE KINGS JEROBOAM AND REHOBOAM AT YOUR FEET!

DID THAT TEACH THEM A LESSON? NO! THE TWO KINGDOMS WENT ON FIGHTING EACH OTHER.

WHAT HAD HAPPENED, DID NOT CHANGE JEROBOAM. SOME TIME LATER HIS SON ABIJAH FELL ILL...

DISGUISE YOURSELF, SO NO ONE WILL RECOGNIZE YOU, AND GO TO SHILOH, TO CONSULT THE PROPHET AHIJAH.

WHEN SHE REACHED AHIJAH'S HOME...

COME IN, WIFE OF JEROBOAM! WHY DO YOU PRETEND TO BE SOMEBODY ELSE? I HAVE BAD NEWS FOR YOU...

THIS IS WHAT THE LORD SAYS TO JEROBOAM: 'I MADE YOU KING OVER MY PEOPLE ISRAEL, BUT YOU HAVE TURNED TO OTHER GODS... ALL YOUR FAMILY WILL BE SWEPT AWAY LIKE DUNG.'

WHEN JEROBOAM'S WIFE RETURNED TO TIRZAH, THE CHILD WAS DEAD...

WHY DID YOU TURN AWAY FROM THE LORD? YOUR WHOLE FAMILY IS GOING TO DIE!

9

AT THE BEGINNING OF THE NINTH CENTURY BC A LITTLE BOY, **'ELI-YAHU** WAS BORN. HIS NAME MEANS 'THE LORD IS GOD.'

MAY HIS LIFE GIVE GLORY TO THE LIVING GOD.

'ELI-YAHU!

MAY HE BRING ISRAEL BACK TO THE LORD!

THERE WAS GREAT JOY IN THE CAMP...

EVERY SON WHO IS BORN IS ONE MORE SERVANT FOR THE LORD.

IT ISN'T A QUESTION OF NUMBERS! ONE IS ENOUGH...

...A PROPHET?

YES... A NEW MOSES!

THE LORD TAKES CARE OF THE GOOD PEOPLE, BUT THE WICKED WILL DIE...

JEROBOAM, BAASHA, OMRI... IT IS ONLY THE NAME THAT CHANGES... BUT NOT ONE OF THEM TURNS BACK TO GOD.

AFTER A REIGN OF ELEVEN YEARS, OMRI DIED, AND **AHAB, HIS SON, BECAME KING.**

AHAB'S WIFE, **JEZEBEL,** WAS A PHOENICIAN PRINCESS. HE WORSHIPPED HER GODS.

LOOK, AHAB! TREES ON THE HILLS, FESTIVALS FOR THE PEOPLE, AND AN IMAGE OF BAAL, WHO GIVES RAIN...

...AND THE WINE WILL BE GOOD, THE OIL WILL BE RICH, AND THERE WILL BE PLENTY OF CORN.

AHAB HAD BEEN KING FOR A FEW YEARS, WHEN ONE DAY...

FRIENDS, I HAVE JUST LEARNED A TERRIBLE THING! JEZEBEL HAS KILLED THE LORD'S PROPHETS, AND AHAB HAS ORDERED THE PEOPLE TO WORSHIP THE BAAL OF PHOENICIA.

I MUST GO AND SPEAK TO THE KING IN THE NAME OF THE LORD!

IN SAMARIA...

AHAB, I BEG YOU, TURN BACK WITH ALL YOUR HEART TO THE LIVING GOD!

ELIJAH, LOOK! FARMS ON EVERY HILL! AND HAVE YOU EVER SEEN FIELDS SO FULL OF WHEAT?

MY GODS ARE JUST AS ALIVE AS YOURS!

WHAT A STRANGE FELLOW!

THE LORD LIVES! THERE WILL BE NO RAIN OR DEW FOR THESE NEXT YEARS, UNTIL I SAY SO.

AND ELIJAH WENT AWAY.

HE WENT TO HIDE BESIDE THE BROOK OF CHERITH, AS THE LORD HAD TOLD HIM.

THE RAVENS BROUGHT HIM HIS FOOD EACH DAY...

BUT VERY SOON THE BROOK RAN DRY.

GO TO ZAREPHATH, NEAR SIDON. A WIDOW WILL FEED YOU.

ALL THIS LONG ROAD – ONLY TO END UP IN PHOENICIA, QUEEN JEZEBEL'S COUNTRY!

Sea

SIDON

ZAREPHATH

PHOENICIA

Mount CARMEL

ISRAEL

Jordan

Mediterranean

SAMARIA

JERUSALEM

Beersheba

JUDAH

NEGEB

I'M RUNNING AWAY FROM KING AHAB LIKE MOSES FLED FROM THE PHARAOH!

NOT FAR FROM ZAREPHATH...

MADAM, I BEG YOU, PLEASE BRING ME SOME WATER AND A PIECE OF BREAD.

I ONLY HAVE ENOUGH TO MAKE ONE LAST CAKE... AFTER EATING THAT, I WILL LIE DOWN BESIDE MY SON...

AND WE WILL WAIT FOR DEATH!

NO! THIS IS WHAT THE LORD, MY GOD, SAYS: 'THE FLOUR WON'T BE USED UP, NEITHER WILL THE OIL, BEFORE I SEND THE RAIN AGAIN?'

ELIJAH STAYED WITH THE WIDOW, AND EVERY DAY THEY HAD ENOUGH TO EAT.

YOUR GOD IS FAITHFUL!

TELL US MORE ABOUT HIM...

IN ISRAEL THE FAMINE WAS SEVERE, AND AHAB SENT MEN TO LOOK FOR ELIJAH ...BUT THEY COULDN'T FIND HIM...

15

A LITTLE WHILE LATER THE WIDOW'S SON FELL ILL AND DIED.

WHY DID YOUR GOD GIVE US LIFE, ONLY TO TAKE IT BACK AGAIN?

GIVE THE CHILD TO ME!

ELIJAH CARRIED THE CHILD INTO HIS BEDROOM.

LORD MY GOD! I BEG YOU: GIVE LIFE BACK TO THIS LITTLE BOY!

LOOK, YOUR SON IS ALIVE!

IT IS YOUR GOD WHO LIVES!

THE DROUGHT HAD LASTED THREE YEARS, WHEN THE LORD TOLD ELIJAH TO LEAVE ZAREPHATH.

I AM BEING CALLED BACK TO ISRAEL... I WILL NEVER FORGET YOU.

WE'LL PRAY FOR YOU!

ISRAEL! ISRAEL! REMEMBER YOUR FATHERS, AND DON'T BE STUBBORN.

AHAB FOUND OUT THAT ELIJAH THE PROPHET HAD COME BACK. HE WENT TO MEET HIM.

SO THERE YOU ARE — THE WORST TROUBLEMAKER IN ISRAEL!

NO! THAT IS YOU! BECAUSE YOU HAVE TURNED YOUR BACK ON THE LORD AND RUN AFTER THE BAALS!

NOW DO WHAT I TELL YOU. ORDER ALL THE PEOPLE OF ISRAEL AND THE PROPHETS OF BAAL TO COME TOGETHER ON **MOUNT CARMEL**...

AHAB HAD NO CHOICE...
HE WAS SURE THAT ONLY ELIJAH COULD BRING THE RAIN AGAIN.

WHAT A PITY WE DIDN'T GET RID OF ELIJAH WITH ALL THE REST OF THE LORD'S PROPHETS.

FIRST LET HIM GIVE US RAIN, THEN...

HOW LONG WILL YOU SIT ON THE FENCE? IF THE LORD IS GOD, FOLLOW HIM! IF BAAL IS GOD, FOLLOW HIM!

WE HEAR WHAT YOU SAY!

PROPHETS OF BAAL, WE WILL EACH PREPARE A SACRIFICE; THEN WE WILL EACH PRAY TO OUR OWN GOD. THE ONE WHO ANSWERS WITH FIRE IS THE ONLY GOD.

THEN THE LORD SENT FIRE DOWN ONTO THE ALTAR...

THE LORD IS GOD!

GOD OF ISRAEL, HAVE MERCY ON US!

...IT BURNT UP THE SACRIFICE, AND DRIED UP THE WATER IN THE TRENCH.

GRAB THE PROPHETS OF BAAL! DON'T LET ANY OF THEM GET AWAY.

THEY WERE ALL KILLED. SO THEY CAME TO THE SAME END AS THE LORD'S PROPHETS WHOM JEZEBEL HAD MASSACRED.

AHAB, YOU CAN STOP FASTING, AND REJOICE WITH THE PEOPLE. THE RAIN WILL SOON BE HERE.

ELIJAH CLIMBED UP TO THE TOP OF MOUNT CARMEL...

MASTER, MASTER! I WANT TO BE YOUR SERVANT!

WHAT IS YOUR NAME, SON?

ELISHA!*

* God brings help.

ELISHA, CLIMB UP TO THE TOP QUICKLY, AND LOOK OUT TO SEA. TELL ME AS SOON AS YOU SEE ANYTHING.

NOTHING, MASTER! STILL NOTHING!

MY GOD, HAVE MERCY ON YOUR PEOPLE.

AND SUDDENLY...

THERE IT IS! A CLOUD! A LITTLE CLOUD!

AND SOON AFTER THAT...

AHAB RACED BACK TO JEZEBEL AT FULL SPEED.

SO! ELIJAH CONVINCED YOU!

YOU WOULDN'T UNDERSTAND.

LOOK HOW IT IS RAINING! THAT WILL BRING MY KINGDOM BACK TO LIFE. ELIJAH DID WHAT YOUR PROPHETS COULDN'T DO!

THAT IS WHY WE MUST GET RID OF HIM!

ELIJAH FEARED FOR HIS LIFE, AND FLED SOUTHWARDS TO THE KINGDOM OF JUDAH.

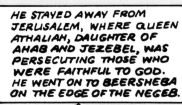

HE STAYED AWAY FROM JERUSALEM, WHERE QUEEN ATHALIAH, DAUGHTER OF AHAB AND JEZEBEL, WAS PERSECUTING THOSE WHO WERE FAITHFUL TO GOD. HE WENT ON TO BEERSHEBA ON THE EDGE OF THE NEGEB.

ELISHA, WE MUST GO FURTHER INTO THE DESERT.

BUT WHY, MASTER? THERE IS NOTHING MORE TO BE AFRAID OF HERE!

THERE! TAKE THE CAKES, GO HOME, AND WAIT THERE FOR ME.

BUT ELIJAH... YOU WILL DIE IN THE DESERT!

I AM ONLY A USELESS SLAVE! I AM NO BETTER THAN MY FATHERS!

AFTER WALKING ALL DAY...

IT IS ENOUGH! NOW, LORD, LET ME DIE.

...HE WAS TIRED OUT, AND HE FELL ASLEEP.

SUDDENLY...

UP WITH YOU! EAT! YOU STILL HAVE A LONG WAY TO GO.

ELIJAH ATE AND DRANK.

ON YOUR WAY! ANOINT HAZAEL KING OF ARAM; ANOINT JEHU KING OF ISRAEL; BUT FIRST ANOINT ELISHA TO BE PROPHET AFTER YOU.

ELIJAH LEFT THERE, AND WENT BACK THROUGH THE DESERT.

AFTER SOME TIME...

COULD I TROUBLE YOU FOR SOME WATER?

...YOU WOULD SAY IT WAS MOSES!

QUICK, BRING HIM A DRINK!

...THEN, ONE DAY...

ELISHA! ELISHA! THERE IS A STRANGER ASKING FOR YOU!

NOW ELISHA WAS WEARING ELIJAH'S GREAT CLOAK.

WHEN HE RETURNED TO HIS FIELD, ELISHA SACRIFICED HIS TWO OXEN.

ELISHA

ELIJAH, THE PROPHET WHO HAD BEEN BANISHED, AND HIS DISCIPLE ELISHA HID A LONG WAY AWAY FROM KING AHAB, WHO STILL REIGNED IN SAMARIA. THOUGH THE ARMY OF ISRAEL HAD DEFEATED THE ARAMAEANS,* THEIR TROOPS ATTACKED AGAIN.

* Also called Syrians.

ELIJAH, IT SEEMS THAT AHAB HAS JUST BEATEN THE ARAMAEANS AGAIN. ON THE PLAIN NEAR APHEK THIS TIME...

THAT VICTORY MUST SURELY COME FROM THE LORD!

SCENARIO: Etienne DAHLER
DRAWING: José BIELSA

AHAB KNOWS THAT! I THINK HE WILL TURN BACK TO GOD NOW.

BUT, ELISHA, YOU ARE FORGETTING THAT AHAB ISN'T ALONE!

JEZEBEL RULES IN HIS HEART, AND SHE GETS ANYTHING SHE WANTS FROM HIM.

IN AHAB'S PALACE IN SAMARIA...

YOU BRAVE SOLDIER! U ARE MORE POWERFUL THAN EVER...

...AND THE PEOPLE SHOULD BE ABLE TO SEE IT! DECORATE YOUR PALACE; ENLARGE YOUR GARDENS.

ACTUALLY, **JEZEBEL**, I WAS JUST THINKING OF BUYING NABOTH'S VINEYARD...

IN NABOTH'S VINEYARD...

I REFUSE! I WON'T GIVE IT UP! IT IS A **SACRED INHERITANCE** FROM MY FATHERS!

JEZEBEL, NABOTH REFUSED TO GIVE ME HIS VINEYARD! ME, THE KING OF ISRAEL!

IT SEEMS THIS NABOTH ISN'T AFRAID OF YOU...

AHAB, YOU LEAVE IT TO ME! YOU WILL HAVE THAT VINEYARD!

PERFECT! PUT THE ROYAL SEAL ON EACH LETTER, AND SEND THEM TO THE LEADING PEOPLE IN THE TOWN.

MY FRIENDS, WHAT DO YOU THINK OF THIS?

WHY DO THAT TO NABOTH? I DON'T UNDERSTAND...

IT IS A CRIME!

IT IS AN ORDER FROM THE KING! ANNOUNCE A FAST, AND BRING NABOTH.

BUT JEZEBEL HIRED TWO FALSE WITNESSES, WHO PUBLICLY ACCUSED NABOTH, JUST AS THE LETTER FROM THE KING COMMANDED.

NABOTH CURSED GOD AND THE KING!

IT IS TRUE. I AM A WITNESS!

THEY FOUND NABOTH GUILTY, AND STONED HIM TO DEATH.

THERE IS NO HOPE FOR ME! I AM LOST!

LORD, HAVE MERCY ON ME!

BECAUSE AHAB HAS HUMBLED HIMSELF, THE DISASTER WON'T HAPPEN WHILE HE IS ALIVE, BUT WHEN HIS SON IS KING.

THEN ELIJAH AND ELISHA WENT BACK TO THEIR HIDING PLACE. THREE YEARS WENT BY WITHOUT WAR BETWEEN ISRAEL AND ARAM. DURING THE THIRD YEAR **JEHOSHAPHAT, KING OF JUDAH,** CAME TO VISIT AHAB.

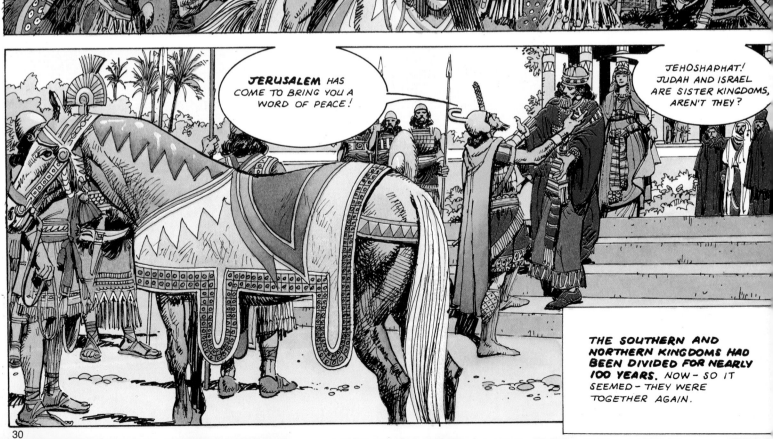

JERUSALEM HAS COME TO BRING YOU A WORD OF PEACE!

JEHOSHAPHAT! JUDAH AND ISRAEL ARE SISTER KINGDOMS, AREN'T THEY?

THE SOUTHERN AND NORTHERN KINGDOMS HAD BEEN DIVIDED FOR NEARLY 100 YEARS. NOW—SO IT SEEMED—THEY WERE TOGETHER AGAIN.

AHAB, YOU HAVE JEHOSHAPHAT, KING OF JUDAH, RIGHT HERE IN YOUR PALACE. IT IS YOUR BEST CHANCE TO BE RID OF HIM.

JEZEBEL, THAT IS IMPOSSIBLE! HE IS LIKE A BROTHER TO ME!

YOU HAVE TO DO IT! HE HAS BROUGHT HIS KINGDOM BACK TO WORSHIP THE LORD... IF YOUR PEOPLE FOLLOW HIS EXAMPLE, WE ARE LOST.

JEZEBEL, YOU ARE RIGHT ONCE MORE... BUT I FEEL AS IF I AM CAUGHT IN A TRAP!

JEHOSHAPHAT, WE BEAT THE ARAMAEANS, BUT THEY STILL HOLD OUR TOWN OF RAMOTH IN GILEAD. WILL YOU FIGHT BESIDE ME TO GET IT BACK?

I AM WITH YOU, AHAB, AND SO IS MY WHOLE ARMY...

... BUT FIRST LET'S ASK THE PROPHETS TO FIND OUT GOD'S WILL.

AHAB CALLED IN HIS PROPHETS...

ATTACK THE TOWN!

GOD WILL DELIVER IT TO YOU!

AHAB, ISN'T THERE A **PROPHET OF THE LORD,** INSTEAD OF THIS LOT WHO SAY ONLY WHAT YOU WANT TO HEAR?

THERE IS STILL MICAIAH, IMLAH'S SON... BUT, JEHOSHAPHAT, HE ONLY PROPHESIES BAD THINGS ABOUT ME...

JEHOSHAPHAT INSISTED THAT MICAIAH BE BROUGHT.

I HAVE SEEN THE PEOPLE OF ISRAEL SCATTERED OVER THE MOUNTAINS LIKE SHEEP WITHOUT A SHEPHERD, AND GOD SAYS: 'THEY NO LONGER HAVE A LEADER; LET THEM ALL GO HOME IN PEACE.'

WHAT DID I TELL YOU, JEHOSHAPHAT?

AS FOR THESE FELLOWS HERE, THE LORD HAS ALLOWED THEM TO TELL LIES!

YOU CHEAT!

THROW HIM INTO PRISON! AND LEAVE HIM THERE UNTIL I COME BACK.

KING AHAB, YOU WILL NEVER COME BACK— **NEVER!**

CAUSE THE PROPHET HAD ONLY SAID THAT E KING OF ISRAEL WOULD BE KILLED, HOSHAPHAT, KING OF JUDAH, DECIDED TAKE PART IN THE BATTLE.

AHAB, DRESS LIKE AN ORDINARY SOLDIER, THEN HEY'LL THINK THAT EHOSHAPHAT IS THE KING OF ISRAEL.

AND IF MICAIAH WAS RIGHT?

THEN THE KING OF JUDAH WILL DIE!

JEZEBEL! I WONDER WHAT THIS TRICK OF YOURS WILL LEAD TO!

ON THE MORNING OF THE BATTLE JEHOSHAPHAT WENT LOOKING FOR AHAB.

HAVE YOU SEEN AHAB, KING OF ISRAEL?

YES, OVER THERE, BUT HE IS DRESSED LIKE AN ORDINARY SOLDIER. YOU WOULDN'T RECOGNIZE HIM. NOR WILL THE ENEMY!

THE TRAITOR! HE WANTS ME TO BE KILLED INSTEAD!

KING JEHOSHAPHAT, WE MUST GET AWAY! THE ENEMY IS ATTACKING!

THE ARAMAEANS QUICKLY SURROUNDED THE MAN THEY THOUGHT WAS THE KING OF ISRAEL, BUT AT THE LAST MOMENT...

THAT ISN'T AHAB! LEAVE THAT MAN! IT IS THE KING OF ISRAEL WE WANT!

DON'T FOLLOW HIM!

LORD MY GOD, SAVE ME! SAVE THE KING OF JUDAH!

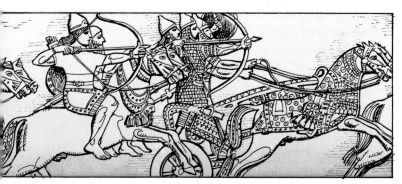

AHAZIAH WAS AFRAID OF ANOTHER ENEMY: ASSYRIA. BUT THE ASSYRIANS WENT BACK HOME WITHOUT ATTACKING ISRAEL. A FEW MONTHS LATER NEW TROUBLE HIT THE COUNTRY.

WHAT HAPPENED?

YOUR MAJESTY, YOUR SON, THE KING, FELL THROUGH THE LATTICE ON HIS BALCONY.

GO AND CONSULT BAAL-ZEBUB, THE GOD OF EKRON, TO SEE IF I WILL LIVE.

ON THE WAY TO EKRON KING AHAZIAH'S MESSENGERS MET ELIJAH AROUND A BEND IN THE ROAD.

DO YOU THINK THERE IS NO GOD IN ISRAEL? IS THAT WHY YOU ARE OFF TO CONSULT BAAL-ZEBUB?

THAT IS WHY THE LORD SAYS TO AHAZIAH: 'YOU WILL NOT LEAVE YOUR BED AGAIN. YOU ARE GOING TO DIE!'

WHEN ELIJAH RETURNED...

THE LORD IS CALLING ME TO JERICHO. **STAY HERE, ELISHA.**

NO, I WON'T LEAVE YOU!

WHEN THEY REACHED THE BANK OF THE JORDAN...

LOOK! THEY'RE CROSSING THE RIVER!

ELIJAH IS GOING BACK TO THE PLACE WHERE MOSES DIED.

ELISHA, TELL ME WHAT YOU WANT ME TO DO FOR YOU BEFORE I AM TAKEN AWAY.

I WOULD LIKE A DOUBLE PORTION* OF YOUR SPIRIT.

* Double portion: what the eldest son inherited when his father died.

THAT IS DIFFICULT! BUT IF YOU SEE ME AS I AM TAKEN AWAY, IT WILL BE GIVEN TO YOU.

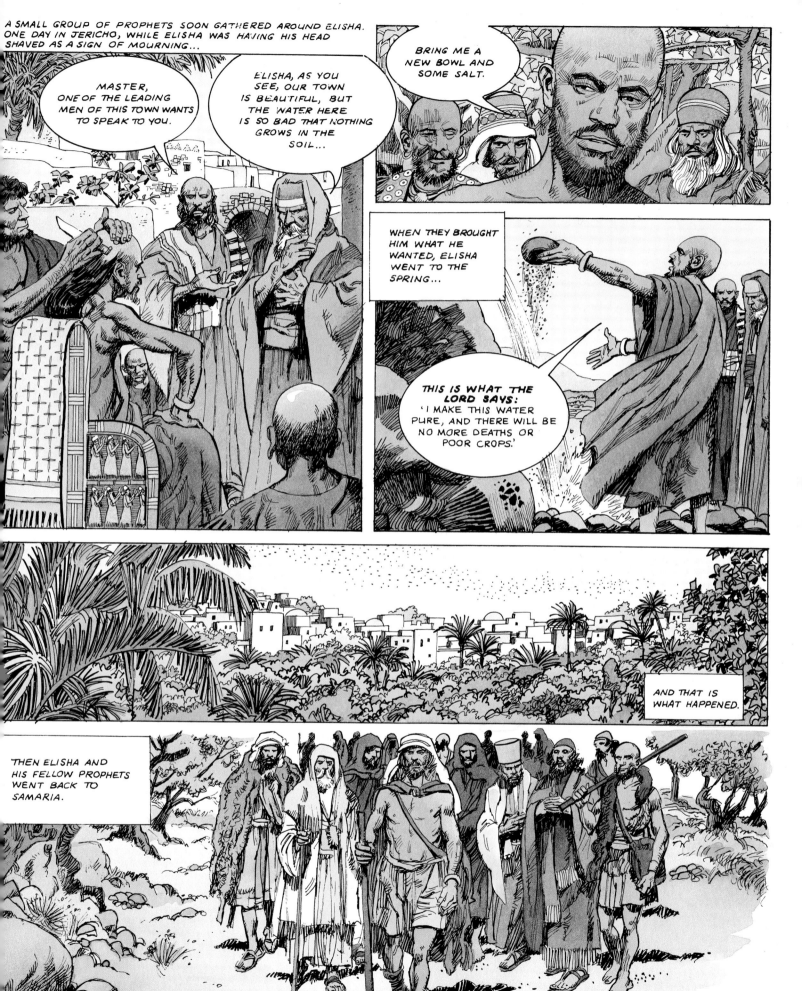

SOON THERE WERE 100 IN THE GROUP.

...THEN THE TRAVELLER SAID TO ABRAHAM, 'WHEN I RETURN IN A YEAR'S TIME, YOU WILL HAVE A SON...'

ELISHA TEACHES US LIKE THIS EVERY DAY, AND GOD SPEAKS TO US THROUGH HIM.

THEY SAY THAT YOUR MASTER WORKS MIRACLES.

IT IS TRUE! LISTEN! ONE DAY THE WIDOW OF ONE OF OUR PROPHETS CAME TO ELISHA...

SHE COULDN'T PAY HER DEBTS, AND THE MAN TO WHOM SHE OWED THE MONEY WAS THREATENING TO TAKE HER SONS AS SLAVES...

WHAT HAVE YOU STILL GOT AT HOME?

NOTHING MORE, ELISHA... ONLY A SMALL JAR OF OIL.

BORROW MANY EMPTY JARS FROM YOUR NEIGHBOURS, AND THEN DO WHAT I TELL YOU...

BACK HOME...

MOTHER, YOU HAVE ALREADY FILLED FIVE JARS WITH YOUR OIL!

QUICKLY! BRING ME THE OTHERS!

ALL THE JARS ARE FULL!

...AND THE OIL HAS STOPPED FLOWING!

SO THE WIDOW WAS ABLE TO SELL THE OIL AND PAY ALL HER DEBTS.

YOUR MASTER REALLY IS A MAN OF GOD!

LET ME TELL YOU ABOUT ANOTHER OF ELISHA'S MIRACLES...

ONE DAY ELISHA AND HIS SERVANT GEHAZI WERE STAYING AT SHUNEM WITH A LADY WHO ALWAYS PUT THEM UP.

GEHAZI, THIS WOMAN IS SO GENEROUS WITH HER HOSPITALITY... I WOULD LIKE TO GIVE HER SOMETHING SHE DEARLY WANTS.

ELISHA, SHE LONGS TO HAVE A SON, BUT HER HUSBAND IS TOO OLD.

LADY, BY THIS TIME NEXT YEAR YOU WILL BE HOLDING A SON IN YOUR ARMS.

OH, SIR, PLEASE LET IT BE TRUE!

EVERYTHING HAPPENED JUST AS ELISHA HAD SAID.

A FEW YEARS WENT BY, AND THEN ONE DAY, WHEN THE LITTLE BOY WAS HELPING HIS FATHER WITH THE HARVEST, HE GOT A TERRIBLE HEADACHE...

DADDY, MY HEAD! MY HEAD!

TAKE HIM HOME TO HIS MOTHER.

THE CHILD SUFFERED FOR AN HOUR OR TWO, BUT AT NOON HE DIED.

MY CHILD! WHY HAS HE BEEN TAKEN AWAY FROM ME?

THEN SHE WENT TO FIND ELISHA. FIRST HE SENT GEHAZI WITH HIS STICK, SO HE COULD TOUCH THE CHILD WITH IT...

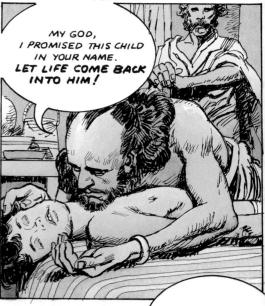

...BUT NOTHING HAPPENED. THEN ELISHA HIMSELF WENT TO THE LITTLE BOY'S BED.

MY GOD, I PROMISED THIS CHILD IN YOUR NAME. LET LIFE COME BACK INTO HIM!

GEHAZI, CALL HIS MOTHER! HE IS ALIVE!

LET'S GO AND SIT WITH THE PROPHET'S OTHER FOLLOWERS. THE MEAL MUST HAVE ALREADY BEGUN.

ALL THESE MIRACLES SEEM VERY STRANGE TO ME...

LISTEN... THE PROPHET ELISHA IS AT WORK IN THE HISTORY OF OUR PEOPLE, BECAUSE THE LORD IS ALSO THE MASTER OF HISTORY.

WHEN ISRAEL AND JUDAH WERE WAGING WAR AGAINST THE MOABITES...

THEY TOOK THE SOUTHERN ROUTE, BUT HAD A VERY HARD TIME IN THE DESERT...

AT THIS RATE WE WILL HAVE NO SOLDIERS LEFT BY THE TIME WE REACH MOAB!

WE MUST ASK GOD TO HELP US! LET'S CONSULT A PROPHET.

THE TWO KINGS WENT TO FIND ELISHA.

I THOUGHT THE KING OF ISRAEL HAD FORGOTTEN GOD! ...BUT BECAUSE I RESPECT THE KING OF JUDAH, I WILL LISTEN TO YOU.

FETCH A MUSICIAN.

WHILE THE MUSICIAN PLAYED, THE POWER OF THE LORD CAME UPON ELISHA...

DIG! DIG DITCHES! THE LORD WILL FILL THEM AND YOU WILL DRINK...

HE WILL DELIVER MOAB INTO YOUR HANDS!

THE TWO KINGS LISTENED TO ELISHA. GOD GAVE THEIR ARMY WATER, AND LET THEM WIN MANY BATTLES.

BUT THAT IS NOTHING TO WHAT HAPPENED AT DAMASCUS IN ARAM!

HAZAEL, A SERVANT OF KING BENHADAD II, WENT TO MEET ELISHA.

MY NAME IS HAZAEL, AND THE KING OF SYRIA, WHO IS ILL, WANTS TO KNOW IF HE WILL GET BETTER.

TELL HIM HE WILL GET BETTER...

... BUT ACTUALLY, HAZAEL, GOD HAS SHOWN ME THAT HE IS GOING TO DIE.

ELISHA, WHY ARE YOU CRYING?

HAZAEL, I KNOW ALL THE TERRIBLE THINGS YOU ARE GOING TO DO TO THE PEOPLE OF ISRAEL, BECAUSE THE LORD HAS SHOWN ME THAT YOU WILL BE KING OF ARAM.

WHEN YOU ARE KING, YOU WILL SLAUGHTER THEIR WARRIORS, BATTER THEIR CHILDREN, AND RIP OPEN THEIR PREGNANT WOMEN!

HAZAEL RUSHED BACK TO THE PALACE IN DAMASCUS...

WELL, WHAT DID THE MAN OF GOD SAY?

THAT YOU WILL GET BETTER.

NOW I AM KING OF ARAM!

THE NEXT DAY HAZAEL SMOTHERED KING BENHADAD, AND SEIZED THE THRONE.

AND GOD STILL HAD OTHER STRANGE THINGS TO SHOW US THROUGH A MAN LIKE ELISHA!

A LITTLE WHILE LATER ELISHA CALLED ONE OF HIS YOUNG COMPANIONS.

TAKE THIS FLASK OF OIL AND GO TO RAMOTH IN GILEAD.

THE ARAMAEANS HELD THE TOWN, WHICH WAS BEING BESIEGED BY THE ARMY OF JORAM, KING OF ISRAEL.

I AM LOOKING FOR A MAN CALLED JEHU...

YOU WON'T HAVE ANY TROUBLE FINDING HIM! HE HAS BEEN IN COMMAND SINCE THE KING WAS WOUNDED AND THEY TOOK HIM BACK TO JEZREEL TO RECOVER.

JEHU, I HAVE SOMETHING TO SAY TO YOU.

TO ME? RIGHT! I AM COMING...

LET'S GO IN HERE. WE WON'T BE DISTURBED.

BUT THE ARAMAEANS WERE NOT ABLE TO PROFIT VERY MUCH FROM THE TROUBLES ABOUT TO BREAK OUT IN ISRAEL...

THE POWERFUL ASSYRIAN ARMY WAS ALREADY ON THE MARCH, HEADED BY SHALMANESER III.

MASTER, I HAVE DONE WHAT YOU TOLD ME TO DO.

AND SO I HAVE FINISHED THE WORK ELIJAH GAVE ME TO DO...

... BUT THE TROUBLES OF ISRAEL AND JUDAH AREN'T OVER!

WHEN THE PROPHET ELISHA'S MESSENGER HAD ANOINTED HIM, JEHU PREPARED TO REMOVE KING JORAM FROM THE THRONE...

JORAM, IT IS BETWEEN THE TWO OF US!

FORWARD!